Fungi

Fungi

By Thomas Huston Macbride

LM Publishers

I.

TOADSTOOLS AND MUSHROOMS

The fungi as a class may hardly be called popular. For various reasons they are, so to speak, under a cloud. They are little known, and so in lieu of better information the legend "poison" seems to run for all the finer and more showy species. If not held absolutely poisonous, most are at least considered useless and are nameless. Literature, the all-embracing, which concerns itself freely with other forms of animate nature, draws a line at the fungi; and Browning evinces great boldness when he ventures to touch with the wand of his poesy "the freaked, fawn-colored, flaky crew" that rises in November hours.

Worse than all this, thanks to the imperfect knowledge of days not long gone by, the very word fungus is uncanny, and to most minds of vague, uncertain application, suggestive of things unpleasant, not to say direful. For what, forsooth, is a fungus?

A wily invader which, having by some unguarded entrance gained access, may do all sorts of mischief; may fill our cellar, for instance, and turn us out of house and home, as one is reputed to have filled the cellar of the wine merchant, barring the door from within and threatening summary eviction and what not! Is it not a fearful parasite which, having found lodging in the tissues of its unwilling host, swells to proportions vast, a hidden tumor, sending its human victim all too soon forth from his tenement of clay?

Even when not thus associated with the destruction of nobler forms, fungi are nevertheless held *suspect*. At best and largest they are odd, peculiar, hiding in out-of-the-way places, far from "the warm precincts of the cheerful day"; "off color," as men say, and owing little or no allegiance to our sovereign sun; pale, ghastly things whose homes are with the dead.

It remained for modern Science to dignify the world; nothing shall be stranger to her touch benign. Even the fungi come into prominence as they come into light. Odd as they may appear and mysterious too, they, like some odd and peculiar people, do greatly improve upon acquaintance. Certainly no one can look in upon a basket of *Boleti* fresh from August woods and not greatly admire their delicate tints, their yellows, purples, browns, and grays. Fungi, once for all, are plants, for the most part very simple ones too; in their larger forms more commonly useful than noxious, and positively sources of serious injury and detriment in those species only which to mankind at large are unseen, unknown, and unsuspected. To these reference will be made again; for the present let us consider such forms only as meet the eye of ordinary observation, the common denizens of forest and of field.

Assuming the vegetable nature of fungi, the most notable thing about them, as compared with all surrounding vegetation, is their color. Growing plants are green; Whitney says the words are synonymous. But whatever the colors fungi may take on, and they are often brilliantly tinted, they are never green, at any rate in the sense of possessing leaf-green. Without exception the fungi are chlorophyl-less. This, though a negative quality, is, nevertheless, a very convenient one, and withal expressive, for it defines exactly the place these plants must hold in the economy of nature.

Chlorophyl, as is well known, gives to ordinary plants their special and peculiar ability, namely, the power to elaborate the most important organic products—starch, sugar, and the like. This power, accordingly, the chlorophyl-less fungi have not. They are strictly non-productive plants; all that they have they receive. Likewise bringing to the feast of life naught save appetite, they must needs lay under contribution, living or dead, the whole organic world, and are *parasites* or *saprophytes* according to their dietary habits. Such as derive their nourishment from dead organic matter are saprophytes, while those which assail living organisms, and derive food-supply direct from the living tissues of living hosts, are properly enough called parasites.

Somehow or other, through sympathy perhaps, we are more willing to pardon saprophytism than parasitism pure and simple, and Nature apparently takes the same view of the case, for the saprophytes include all the largest and finest specimens of the fungus kind.

Mushrooms, toadstools, earth-stars, puff-balls, stink-horns, truffles, bracket-fungi, are nearly without exception saprophytes. Such fungi, too, as we see, have won attention and enjoy something of a popular classification. This classification science largely confirms — not wholly; and it is interesting to notice that it is just where the popular classification is weak that science fails to discover difference. Many a country wight and many an epicure as well would deem it rare fortune could he learn to distinguish invariably toadstools from mushrooms. Suppose we say that toadstools are poisonous while mushrooms are not.

A toadstool, accordingly, is a poisonous mushroom, and a mushroom is an edible toadstool. The only possible means, therefore, by which the two may be distinguished is a test direct, as in the old rule which bids the inquirer eat with the assurance that, if he survive, he has eaten a mushroom; if he die, a toadstool. But some species»poisonous to one person are by no means so to another; so that even the rule just quoted is unsatisfactory on the score of being inconclusive, as well as inconvenient of application.

Even *Agaricus muscarius,* esteemed so very poisonous to ordinary mortals, is said to produce in the Kamtchatkan simply an increase of that pleasing stupidity which the Chinaman seeks in his opium-bowl or the American in his beer. Furthermore, Science runs her lines not as between toadstools and mushrooms, but as between specific forms. Poisonous and not poisonous, edible and inedible, are side by side in any enumeration of species. Let it be once known which are edible species, and these may thereafter be readily recognized by any one competent to discern a species—no easy matter, by the way, even to the practiced student.

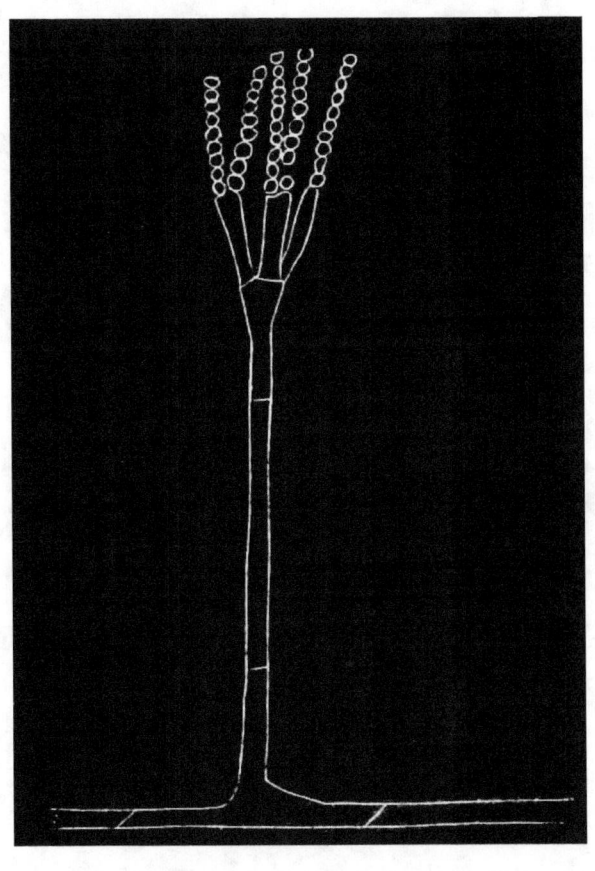

FIG. 1.—FRUIT OF GREEN MOLD (*Penicillium glaucum*).

So much for popular estimate and classification. Let us now briefly consider fungi from the standpoint of structure, the true basis of classification or distinction. A bit of mold placed on the stage of our microscope will enable us to make a beginning (Fig. 1).

Here we have cells, of course, tubular in shape and disposed to form thread-like branches in different directions. These threads are known as *hyphæ,* and fungi generally are masses of hyphæ modified here and there to the accomplishment of various functions. Fungi, like other organisms, have two principal things to do, to accumulate energy and to expend it; to grow and to produce fruit. The hyphæ of a fungus are, therefore, in ordinary cases of two sorts — nutrient hyphæ forming the mycelium, and fruiting hyphæ which make up the fructification. In what we term puff-ball, mushroom, we have simply the fructification — the fruiting hyphæ — all compacted together, while the mycelium lies hidden beneath the surface. When, however, we pluck the mushroom from its place, the mycelium may perhaps seldom be discovered.

There are for this two reasons: first, the mycelial threads are generally tenuous and delicate in the extreme, and unless crowded together escape observation; and, secondly, once the fructification or colony of mushrooms is formed, the energy of the mycelium having passed above the surface, the threads vanish. Only in special cases, or where the fructification is unusually large, and the number of hyphæ converging at a single point in consequence very great, do we find root-like structures that are at once obvious and persistent. Fugacious as the mycelium thus appears, it is really in many—perhaps most—cases much longer-lived than the fructification it creates. Months—possibly in some instances years—elapse while the subterranean hyphal threads ramifying and spreading through myriad diminutive tunnels are ingathering to some single center those resources of nutriment and energy which shall at length break forth with a suddenness and volume utterly astounding.

In my neighbor's yard, not long ago, appeared a succession of giant puff-balls one after another, sometimes two or three at a time, over an area of perhaps thirty by forty feet. In size the plants ranged from the dimensions of a goose-egg to that of a half-bushel, and the amount of matter raised above the surface was little less than one hundred pounds. The largest fruit seemed simply sessile, hardly attached to the substratum, while others, smaller, showed something like a tap-root, white, cord-like, extending a few inches downward—not a root, certainly, rather the undeveloped base of the ball itself. Whence had all this wealth of organic matter come, and what was the meaning of it all?

The previous existence of a wood-yard on the locality affords probable explanation of the phenomenon. Through and through the accumulated detritus of the old wood-yard the mycelium of the puff-ball had literally threaded its way, developing perchance for years over an area of not less than twelve hundred square feet, restoring again for the moment to the kingdom of life and light organic matter which seemed fallen into ruin irretrievable.

Turning our attention now to the fructification, we shall find our mushroom to consist of the following parts: A short stalk. or stem, crowned with a cap, the *pileus.* This cap consists of an expanded disk, bearing on its lower surface hundreds of radiating plates, the gills or lamellæ, with sharp edges and delicately tinted, velvety sides. Cut a section perpendicular to the course of these plates or gills, and we have a comb-like structure which under a good lens presents the appearance portrayed in Fig. 2.

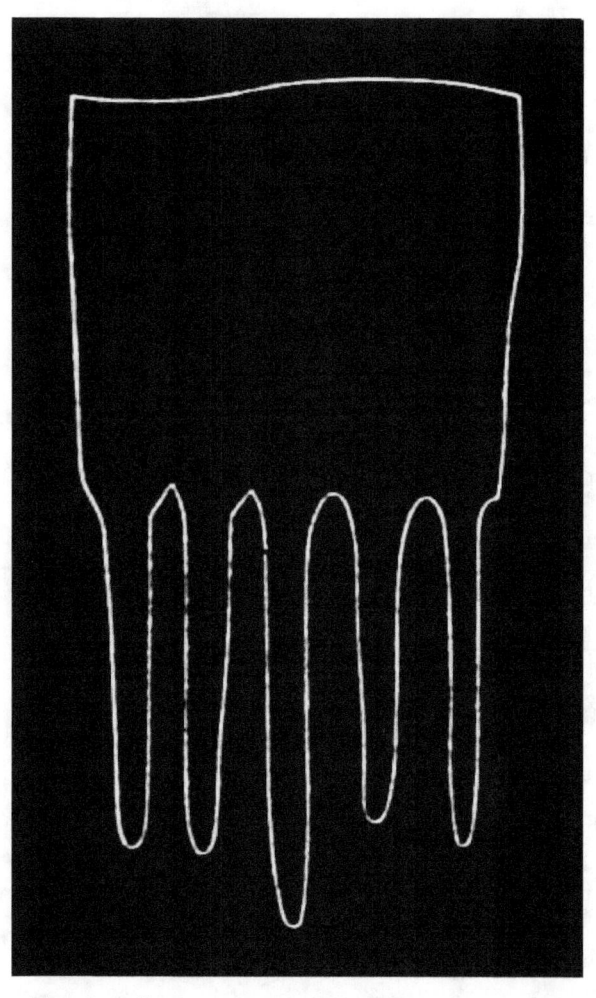

FIG. 2.—SECTION OF THE LAMELLÆ OF COMMON MUSHROOM.

Under still better lenses we may discover on each gill-section a marginal row of rather large cylindric cells, each bearing at its summit a pair of smaller cells manifestly formed by abstriction from diverging branches of the larger cell (see Fig. 3).

The small cells are the spores, and the supporting cell but the terminus of an extended and much-branched hypha, which has blended with a myriad like itself to form stalk and cap and gill of our completed mushroom. That is the whole structure, and yet from such simple machinery behold what wealth and variety of form and style come forth! Other modes of spore-production there are to be hereafter seen, but that described is characteristic cross-section. of the vast majority of those greater fungi which occupy the shadows of our world. To begin with, there are hundreds of species of